M000119826

ALSO BY STEDMAN GRAHAM

You Can Make It Happen

YOU
CAN MAKE IT HAPPEN
EVERY DAY

Stedman Graham

Rev. DARYL
Williams

Enjoy

Stedman
Graham

A FIRESIDE BOOK

Published by Simon & Schuster

FIRESIDE
Rockefeller Center
1230 Avenue of the Americas
New York, NY 10020

Copyright © 1998 by Stedman Graham

All rights reserved, including the right of reproduction
in whole or in part in any form.

FIRESIDE and colophon are registered trademarks of Simon & Schuster Inc.

Designed by Pagesetters/IPA

Manufactured in the United States of America

1   3   5   7   9   10   8   6   4   2

Library of Congress Cataloging-in-Publication Data

Graham, Stedman.
You can make it happen every day / Stedman Graham.
p.   cm.
"A Fireside book."
1. Success—Psychological aspects—Quotations, maxims, etc.   I. Title.
BF637.S8G684   1998
158.1—dc21   98-16526
CIP
ISBN 0-684-84322-6

This book is dedicated to Jan Miller, my literary agent, a true professional with a big heart and a strong vision; Carolyn Reidy, whose leadership at Simon & Schuster made it possible for me to deliver a message I believe in; and Dominick Anfuso, my editor, who makes it happen every day through his determination and genuine spirit.

A key element of the success process is nurturing relationships with those who believe in you and your goals. W. E. B. Du Bois said it better than I can: "Self-realization would not be achieved one by one, but all together or not at all."

CONTENTS

FOREWORD

THE STEPS TO SUCCESS outlined in this book are the culmination of years of self-examination, reflection, and trial and error. *You Can Make It Happen Every Day* is meant to guide and encourage you as you make your own journey through the Nine-Step Plan for Success detailed in my book *You Can Make It Happen*.

One lesson that stands apart in my personal adventure was recently expressed most eloquently by an acquaintance delivering a public address: "No one branch bears fruit by itself." Behind every individual success is a network of people who make that victory possible: family and friends who provide emotional and personal assistance; co-workers who challenge you to achieve more or make those achievements possible by providing support; and many, many people who have a stake—emotional, financial, or societal—in your success.

9

For most of my life I was, like most people, unaware that there could a process for pursuing success. As a result, life lived me for years, as I took what came to me rather than taking myself where I wanted to go. After years of contemplation, I came to understand that I needed to develop a vision and plan for where I wanted to go in my life. Equipped with this understanding, I had the base from which I could branch out, going after my dreams for a better life: I had begun the Success Process.

No matter where your life is, if you are willing to undertake a systematic pursuit of a better life, it is within your reach. As you follow my Nine-Step Plan, you will learn a great deal about yourself, and you may discover, as I did, that the biggest obstacles to your pursuit of a better life come from within. I learned to overcome past injuries and prejudices and to build a positive self-image; I had to take control of the everyday circumstances we all face and assume responsibility for my future. The Success Process will help you gain the self-knowledge you need to overcome barriers to personal growth, freeing you to pursue your vision of a better life.

Until we look beyond forces that have acted upon us and see ourselves—our conscious and our unconscious—as the principal forces in our lives, we won't overcome our limitations. As you read, don't allow your circumstances to be a factor; consider only the possibilities and the opportunities. *You* decide where you are going, when you are going, and how you are going to get there. And when you get where you want to go, commit to reaching the next level of accomplishment and continue that upward journey in making it happen for yourself.

The steps outlined in this book are trail markers that should help you keep on track in your quest for a more satisfying and rewarding job, a more balanced personal life, and a meaningful role in your community. Refer to this pocketbook daily. Read each step carefully and reflect on how each can be applied to every aspect of your life. Record your vision, goals, values, and principles and refer to them regularly to be sure you never stray too far from the path and always move forward.

You *can* make it happen every day. With an open heart, an open mind, dedication, perseverance, and hard work. Good luck on your journey.

—STEDMAN GRAHAM

I f one advances confidently in the direction of his dreams, and endeavors to live the life which he has imagined, he will meet with a success unexpected in common hours.

—HENRY DAVID THOREAU

STEP 1:
CHECK YOUR ID

>>>>>>>>>>>

Increasing Self-Awareness

There is something in every one of you that waits and listens for the sound of the genuine in yourself. It is the only true guide you will ever have. And if you cannot hear it, you will all of your life spend your days on the ends of strings that somebody else pulls.

—HOWARD THURMAN

None of us are defined by our circumstances, nor are we defined by how other people perceive us. It is up to each one of us to define ourselves, and that is a life's work.

Each of us has the ability to lead a dynamic life by pursuing our unique goals and dreams. There are no limits to what you can accomplish when you know who you are and have faith in what you can do.

—STEDMAN GRAHAM

My contemplation of life ... taught me that he who cannot change the very fabric of his thought ... will never be able to change reality, and will never, therefore, make any progress.

—ANWAR SADAT

At some point in our lives, most of us need help in overcoming whatever it is that is holding us back, whether it is racism, sexism, elitism, or any of the obstacles that stand between you and your dreams and aspirations.

Self-knowledge is where success begins. The first step in developing fundamental *self-awareness* is to examine the things that influence your behavior, both those that hold you back and those that push you to pursue a better life. This understanding gives you the power to change and control your behavior in a more positive and effective manner.

—SG

Somehow I can't believe that there are any heights that can't be scaled by a man who knows the secret of making dreams come true. This special secret, it seems to me, can be summarized in four c's. They are curiosity, confidence, courage, and constancy, and the greatest of these is confidence. When you believe in a thing, believe in it all the way, implicitly and unquestionably.

—WALT DISNEY

If you want to create a vision for your life and then follow that vision, you must have *confidence*. You have to feel that you deserve success. People with positive self-images believe in themselves, in their abilities, and in their power to control their own lives. You gain confidence by concentrating on the talents and attributes and personal history that make you special and unique.

—SG

We cannot afford to settle for being just average; we must learn as much as we can to be the best that we can. The key word is education— that's knowledge—education with maximum effort.

—BILL COSBY

»»»»»»»»»»

You must acquire the knowledge, training, and skills to find solutions to the life problems you encounter and to find the process for success. You develop *competence* by slowly building upon your skills, first in one area and then another, through hard work and perseverance.

—SG

Plant the seeds of expectation in your mind; cultivate thoughts that anticipate achievement. Believe in yourself as being capable of overcoming all obstacles and weaknesses.

—NORMAN VINCENT PEALE

You must feel *capable* of defining, creating, and controlling your life. You can do this by working on your self-discipline, by making a list of personal goals and objectives. Start with something small, do it, and then challenge yourself to do something else. As you master each of these small goals and objectives, over time you will work up to much bigger ones, proving to yourself and others that you have the power to control your life.

—SG

Opportunity is limitless. Where there is an open mind, there will always be a frontier.

—CHARLES F. KETTERING

When you have a sense of your own identity and a vision of where you want to go in your life, you then have the basis for reaching out to the world and going after your dreams. Most of those who succeed in achieving their goals do it by creating an environment for opportunity. They open themselves to positive change by becoming positive, energized people. They believe in themselves, giving others cause to believe in them.

—SG

STEP 2:
CREATE YOUR
VISION

Deciding What You Want for Your Life
Through Your Dreams and Aspirations

Lift up yourselves . . . take yourselves out of the mire and hitch your hopes to the stars.

—FREDERICK DOUGLASS

You cannot be successful if you have no vision or if you don't feel worthy of success. A lack of vision inhibits your development and growth as a person. Look at the qualities that you bring to the table and the interests that you have so that you can *develop a vision* of where you want to go in life. This is your life's destination. It is where you want to go in your journey through the Success Process.

—SG

The road to happiness lies in two simple principles: Find what it is that interests you and that you can do well, and when you find it put your whole soul into it—every bit of energy and ambition and natural ability you have.

—JOHN D. ROCKEFELLER

Your talents are your gifts. If you develop your talents, people and resources will come to you. Often, you express your talents so naturally that you may not recognize them. What you love to do is generally what you naturally do well.

Get in the habit of regularly thinking of the possibilities for you and your talents. Open your mind and expand your vision of where those talents can take you and how you can build your life by doing what you love to do.

—SG

F*ind a purpose in life so big it will challenge every capacity to be at your best.*

—DAVID O. MCKAY

Once you have decided what talents and interests you want to engage in your pursuit of a better life, you must form a vision around them. *Use your imagination to create your reality.* Envision the possibility of something that is not only desirable but attainable, based on who you are and where you can go in life.

—SG

*G*oals *give you the specific direction to take to make your dreams come true.*

—BOB CONKLIN

⟫⟫⟫⟫⟫⟫⟫⟫⟫⟫➤

The next step is to set goals that will serve as stepping-stones toward fulfillment of your vision. Your goals are extensions of your vision for your life and reflections of your talents and interests and values.

A primary purpose for setting goals is to get you moving in the right direction. When you set goals, you have to keep them always in mind. Without focus, you lose power and direction.

—SG

The primary purpose of goal-setting is to pull change in the direction you have chosen—one which fits your expertise and overall plan.

—JIM TUNNEY

Goals must be realistic. Just as your vision for a better life should be well grounded in reality rather than fantasy, your goals must be attainable as well as designed to build gradually. Goals must be meaningful and well defined. They should follow a natural progression to a target locked in your mind.

—SG

W*e need to remember that we are created creative and can invent new scenarios as frequently as they are needed.*

—MAYA ANGELOU

Realistically, things can happen as you pursue your vision of a better life, so your goals may require fine-tuning along the way. You may accomplish some easier than you had thought; others may elude you. Keep your vision in mind and make adjustments as you go in order to stay on target.

—SG

STEP 3:
DEVELOP YOUR
TRAVEL PLAN

>>>>>>>>>>>>>

Choosing Action Steps Toward Your Goals

Whether or not you reach your goals in life depends entirely on how well you prepare for them and how badly you want them.... You're eagles! Stretch your wings and fly to the sky!

—RONALD MCNAIR

〉〉〉〉〉〉〉〉〉〉〉

If you're to fulfill your vision for a better life, you must *formulate a plan of action*. Effective planning involves identifying and prioritizing those actions that will move you most efficiently toward your goal.

—SG

You are free to choose, but the choices you make today will determine what you will have, be, and do in the tomorrow of your life.

—ZIG ZIGLAR

Each of us has limited time, energy, and resources, so it is not possible to do everything that might move us toward our goals. Deciding which steps to take can be difficult, but if you weigh your choices carefully, you can take great strides with a few efficient steps rather than running all over the place trying to do too much.

—SG

N othing splendid has ever been achieved ex-
cept by those who dared believe that something inside them was superior to circumstance.

—BRUCE BARTON

When you set goals and achieve them by following a plan, you create a certain *magic* by building confidence in your own value and worthiness. You begin to live out of your imagination, looking forward to the possibilities for your life rather than backward at the limitations and liabilities of your past.

—SG

D̲o not let what you cannot do interfere with what you can do.

—JOHN WOODEN

It is just as important to know what *not* to do as what to do. It is important not to back down when faced with challenges or hard times as you follow your vision, but it is equally important that you don't waste time on things you cannot control. Focus on the things that you *can* change in order to achieve your goals.

—SG

*M*ost *barriers to your success are man-made.*
And most often, you're the man who made
them.

—FRANK TYGER

Don't procrastinate. Putting things off is a terrible habit that is the result of not staying focused on what is truly important. Procrastination is a by-product of fear. It is a protective mechanism for those who want to stay within a certain comfort zone. It is very detrimental to any kind of advancement.

—SG

If you want to make good use of your time, you've got to know what's most important and then give it all you've got.

—LEE IACOCCA

Every day, do something that is truly important in moving you toward your goals. You must choose to invest your time in the important steps. When you take charge of your time, you take charge of your life. How you spend your time reflects your priorities. When you have trouble taking the steps to reach a goal, you need to explore whether the goal really reflects your deepest needs, desires, and values—your true priorities in life.

—SG

STEP 4:
MASTER THE RULES
OF THE ROAD

*Overcoming Adversity Through
Determination and Perseverance*

There is no easy walk to freedom anywhere and many of us will have to pass through the valley of the shadow of death again and again before we reach the mountaintop of our desires.

—NELSON MANDELA

Life is a journey we travel one day at a time. Day by day and step by step, you have to maintain your vigilance and hold on to your vision for your life no matter what happens around you or to you. To get where we want to go in life, we have to keep at it. We have to create a vision, make choices based on what moves us most swiftly toward our goals, and go after them with determination and single-mindedness. And whenever you encounter a problem, no matter how insurmountable it might seem, there is one simple response that should be ingrained in your behavior: Never give up.

—SG

I n life you are as small as your controlling desire
or as great as your dominant aspiration.

—ARMSTRONG WILLIAMS

Let your *conscience* be your guide. Your conscience is the inner voice that serves as a quality-control check on your actions. It monitors your actions and attempts to keep them in line with your belief system. Develop your conscience and learn to tune in to it effectively as you develop a plan to pursue your vision.

—SG

To succeed, we must have the will to succeed, we must have stamina, determination, back-bone, perseverance, self-reliance, and faith.

—B. C. FORBES

Tap into your willpower. Your *will* gives you the power to respond to your conscience rather than to outside influences and distractions. Your will also keeps you going even when the going gets tough, because it holds you to your long-term vision, blocking out short-term distractions. You can add muscle to your willpower by working hard at keeping your promises, both those you make to yourself and those you make to others.

—SG

I *have discovered in life that there are ways of getting almost anywhere you want to go, if you really want to go.*

—LANGSTON HUGHES

It is also necessary to be imaginative in planning actions to achieve your goals. Your *ingenuity* allows you to keep your goals in mind, to see ahead, beyond your present situation and circumstances, to the day when you have fulfilled your vision for your life. It also helps you to search for and find *ingenious* solutions to problems that you will encounter along the way.

—SG

V alues are *guiding devices to enhance our ability to achieve our purposes.*

—ALLAN COX

Before putting into action your plans for pursuing a better life, you need to prepare your own personal Rules of the Road. These rules should be based on the values and principles that you have chosen to guide your life. They are to be guidelines to help you stay on the true course to your goals and give you the strength and determination to fight and overcome distractions, hardships, and obstacles.

Characteristics such as honesty, hard work, a positive attitude, considered thought, and leadership are "Rules" that can be applied to guiding your life.

—SG

I don't sing a song unless I feel it. The song don't tug at my heart, I pass on it. I have to believe in what I'm doing.

—RAY CHARLES

⟫⟫⟫⟫⟫⟫⟫⟫⟫⟫

Refer to your Rules of the Road as you take action on your goals. Check them if you feel your life has lost balance. Keep in mind also that while you should be goal-oriented, it is important not to lose sight of the things you value in life. Maintain a balance between work and family, between family and recreation, between recreation and education, between education and experience.

—SG

STEP 5:
STEP INTO THE
OUTER LIMITS

>>>>>>>>>>>>>>>>

*Taking the Risks Necessary
to Move Forward*

T he guy who takes a chance, who walks the line between the known and unknown, who is unafraid of failure, will succeed.

—GORDON PARKS

Pursuing your dreams requires you to leave your established comfort zone and to push into areas where at first you may feel that you have less control. When you set out on your journey along the Success Process, you have to be willing to grow, to push your talents to the outer limits. That means pushing beyond what is known to you, taking risks, and learning to view failure as merely a step, rather than a defeat.

—SG

By exposing yourself to risk, you're exposing yourself to heavy-duty learning, which gets you on all levels. It becomes a very emotional experience as well as an intellectual experience. Each time you make a mistake, you're learning from the school of hard knocks, which is the best education available.

—GIFFORD PINCHOT

Risk takers are courageous people with the mental and moral strength to take on their fears. They have a *can-do* attitude that is essential for taking risks. People with this attitude understand that failure is not the end of the road. They realize that in failure you can learn how to succeed and grow. The lessons we learn from things that don't work help us to discover those things that do work.

—SG

Progress *is a nice word. But change is its motivator and change has its enemies.*

—ROBERT F. KENNEDY

Thinking about your willingness to take risks helps you focus on what you need to do to get on track to pursue your goals. You have to be prepared to take risks and to try new approaches in order to keep moving along the Success Process. A key lesson here is that *if you continue to do what you have always done, you will continue to get the same result you have always gotten. But if you take well-calculated risks by changing your approach, you can make great progress.*

—SG

If you expect somebody else to guide you, you'll be lost.

—JAMES EARL JONES

Your ability to take risks successfully depends largely on your decision-making skills and also in your approach to risk taking. If you're uncertain of your goals and unclear in your vision for your life, then you are ill prepared to take risks that will move you toward that goal. *If you take a risk for the wrong reasons, you may be sabotaging yourself.* So it is best to measure that risk against your principles, values, and beliefs before you make the leap.

—SG

F*ear is an illusion.*

—MICHAEL JORDAN

The most important risks to take are those that will move you most quickly toward your goals. Take time to carefully evaluate the risks you take so that you can take them with a certain amount of confidence. One thing that is necessary, though, is to overcome any doubts and fears you might have. You cannot live your life out of fear of what might happen. You must live out of your vision for a better life. The greatest reason people do not take risks is fear of the unknown.

—SG

*L*ose not courage, lose not faith, go forward.

—MARCUS GARVEY

We all have fears. Fears are real only when we make them real by investing too much in them. When we allow fear to dominate our lives, we give it too much power.

The only real cure for fear is faith and courage. Fears can haunt and control us when we lack faith in our ability to overcome them and the courage to take them on. Fear defeats us when we allow it to condition our minds, to make us cowards.

—SG

STEP 6:
PILOT THE SEASONS
OF CHANGE

*Managing Your Responses to Changes
Brought On by Taking Risks*

People can't live with change if there's not a changeless core inside them. The key to the ability to change is a changeless sense of who you are, what you are about, and what you value.

—STEPHEN R. COVEY

Learning how to *create and manage your response to change* is crucial if you are going to pursue the Success Process. We all have to learn to welcome, accept, and even bring about change as a natural part of the process of bettering our lives. To do that, you have to *be resilient.* And you have to be patient with the process of change, understanding that it will be accompanied by periods of sadness, disorientation, and even a lack of apparent progress as you adjust to your new circumstances.

—SG

The individuals who will succeed and flourish will also be masters of change: adept at reorienting their own and others' activities in untried directions to bring about higher levels of achievement. They will be able to acquire and use power to produce innovation.

—ROSABETH MOSS KANTER

The first step in learning to master change is accepting that change is not an *event*—it is a *natural process*, like the change of seasons in nature. Each change in seasons occurs in a predictable sequence, and each involves steps that must be completed in order to move to the next level of transition. The process of change is similar.

—SG

If we don't change, we don't grow. If we don't grow, we are not really living. Growth demands a temporary surrender of security.

—GAIL SHEEHY

The emotions and feelings associated with fall are very similar to those commonly experienced in the *letting go* stage of change in our lives. There is a certain excitement and rejuvenation at the changes coming, but also a melancholy over acknowledging that the period marks an ending as well. It is not easy to let go of what has been comfortable and familiar. However, our personal growth can come only when we let go of old ways and self-defeating behavior that has held us back from bettering our lives.

—SG

We cannot become what we need to be by remaining what we are.

—MAX DE PREE

After we let go of our past circumstances, it is common to feel a lingering sadness and a loss of direction. Much like winter, this stage of change sparks images of thoughtfulness and contemplation. This is a time for *reflection*. Use this period to sort out feelings and reflect on your needs, values, and desires while gathering strength and resolve for a new beginning.

—SG

T he business of expanding your consciousness is
   not an option. Either you are expandable or
you are expendable.

—ROBERT SCHULLER

»»»»»»»»➤

Spring inspires a sense of anticipation, of eagerness and high energy. Similarly, this *blossoming* period in the change process can involve rejuvenation and accelerated growth that may be both exciting and a bit frightening. This period requires thoughtful handling. Otherwise you can get swept away by all of the rapid developments and lose focus or feel overwhelmed.

—SG

To exist is to change; to change is to mature; to mature is to create oneself endlessly.

—HENRI BERGSON

In nature, summer is the season in which plants reach *mature* growth. The same holds true for this final stage in the process of change in your life. This is when your preparation and experience bear fruit and sprout the seeds that will guarantee long-term growth. Use this time to reflect on the opportunities that have opened up for you and to evaluate them carefully so that you can choose those that are most in line with your vision.

—SG

STEP 7:
BUILD YOUR
DREAM TEAM

>>>>>>>>>>>>>>

Forging Positive Partnerships to Assist You
in Dealing with Changes in Your Life

Self-realization would not be achieved one by one, but all together or not at all.

—W. E. B. Du Bois

We all need help in dealing with troubles and problems that we encounter as we try to better our lives. Building and maintaining mutually supportive relationships is essential if you are to successfully pursue a better life.

There are few things more valuable and more helpful in your journey along the Success Process than having a support team of trusted friends and family members.

—SG

Integrity is the glue that holds our way of life together.

—BILLY GRAHAM

How do you build and attract members to your support team as you work to create a better life for yourself? You start by proving your *trustworthiness* to others. Trust is not easily earned. Real trust is established over time through shared experiences and a pattern of reliability.

When your actions follow your words, you don't have to work to impress people or win them over. In time, they will see the strength of your character and line up to be on your support team.

—SG

We are inevitably our brother's keeper because we are our brother's brother. Whatever affects one directly affects all indirectly.

—MARTIN LUTHER KING, JR.

People on winning teams share common expectations about appropriate behavior by all of those involved. This includes agreement about such things as what each of the parties can depend on the others for, how personal their conversations will be, what role each member of the team is expected to play, and so on.

—SG

No one can develop freely in this world and find a full life without feeling understood by at least one person.

—PAUL TOURNIER

People involved in successful partnerships have a clear understanding of what part each will play in achieving their mutually agreed-upon goals. Clarity about roles is essential. It gives those involved on your team the information they need about how each fits into the game plan, what they can expect from one another, and how their roles interact.

—SG

A *house divided against itself cannot stand.*

—ABRAHAM LINCOLN

≫≫≫≫≫≫≫≫≫≫≫≫≫

Whenever two or more individuals are engaged in a relationship, disagreements are likely to occur. The challenge in building your team and the relationships within it is to find ways of resolving differences of opinion or other conflicts so that the relationships and the team always move forward, rather than getting hung up on internal problems. Develop a shared plan for confronting and solving problems.

—SG

We all have something to give. So if you know how to read, find someone who can't. If you've got a hammer, find a nail. If you're not hungry, not lonely, not in trouble—seek out someone who is.

—GEORGE BUSH

While building your support team, become part of the support team for someone who may be a few steps back or just starting out behind you. Do not become so focused on your own journey that you cannot stop occasionally and help others along the way. Each of us can make a great difference in the lives of other people, particularly as we move along the Success Process ourselves, growing in strength, gaining experience and knowledge.

—SG

STEP 8:
WIN BY A
DECISION

>>>>>>>>>>>>>

Making Wise Decisions

I ndecision is debilitating; it feeds upon itself; it is, one might almost say, habit-forming.

—HARRY A. HOPF

If you can't bring yourself to make decisions and to take action, you will never be able to break free and create opportunities where none appear to exist.

To make difficult decisions wisely, it helps to have a systematic *process* for assessing each choice and its consequences— the potential impact on each aspect of your life. Having a process will help you make decisions that are consistent with your values and principles as well as your vision for a better life.

—SG

Next to knowing when to seize an opportunity, the most important thing in life is to know when to forgo an advantage.

—BENJAMIN DISRAELI

The need to make a big and important decision generally becomes apparent after you have been exposed to information or an opportunity that somehow sheds new light or gives you a new perspective on your existing situation. This new information or perspective forces you to examine your situation and to *weigh* it in comparison with the possibilities of making a change.

—SG

To raise new questions, new possibilities, to regard old problems from a new angle, requires creative imagination.

—ALBERT EINSTEIN

The next step in the decision-making process is to identify as many suitable alternative solutions or courses of action as possible. This is another stop in the Success Process where it is useful to let your imagination run wild, dreaming up as many possible solutions as you can, weighing them all, and picking and choosing those that might appear to work.

—SG

Have the daring to accept yourself as a bundle of possibilities and undertake the game of making the most of your best.

—HENRY EMERSON FOSDICK

Once you have identified a wide rage of suitable alternatives, mentally try each one on and check to see which best fits your vision for a better life. This is a time to more carefully examine each alternative, to get a feel for and evaluate the pros and cons of each. Make sure you examine them for both the short term and the long term.

—SG

Our lives are a sum total of the choices we have made.

—WAYNE DYER

After identifying the alternative, or alternatives if you are torn between a number of choices, imagine yourself taking that course and take time to consider all of the implications. Anticipate what might happen if you take this route with your life; what will the effect be on your personal relationships, your career, your place in the community? Will it move you along toward your vision for a better life?

—SG

To mobilize yourself, decide what you want, determine what will get you what you want, then act—do what will get you what you want most to achieve.

—NIDO QUBEIN

Once you have committed to making a decision that you have carefully evaluated, you should be prepared to take it all the way without retreating. It is important to know going into it that there will be times when your decision will be challenged, but if you have followed each step in the process and given careful thought to your choices along the way, you should be able to face these challenges and overcome them.

—SG

STEP 9:
COMMIT TO
YOUR VISION

>>>>>>>>>>>>>>>>>>>

*Pledging Your Time and Energy to
the Pursuit of a Better Life*

T hings do not happen. Things are made to happen.

—JOHN F. KENNEDY

»»»»»»»»»»»

The final step in the Success Process is to make a *total commitment* to your vision for a better life and the all-out pursuit of it.

A commitment is not some vague promise to yourself that you will do something. A commitment is something you *live*. Everything you do is a reflection of your commitment. Every approach you take to your life, the good times and the hard times, is an expression of that commitment.

—SG

Now is not the time to cling to what was, but to amend what is.

—HELEN HAYES

Commitment is a capacity for setting goals and achieving them. That capacity can be enlarged only through exercising your power to make commitments and fulfilling them. When you keep your commitments, you build trust in yourself and with others. Commitments are promises, and each commitment that you make and stick with is a goal achieved. Each goal that you achieve is another indication that you are guided by the possibilities of your life, rather than the circumstances.

—SG

S uccess has a price tag on it, and the tag reads COURAGE, DETERMINATION, DISCI-PLINE, RISK TAKING, PERSEVERANCE, and CONSISTENCY—doing the RIGHT THINGS for the RIGHT REASONS and not just when we feel like it.

—JAMES M. MESTON

Commit to success by earning it and knowing that you deserve it. Prepare yourself so that when success comes, you are comfortable with it. Learn to celebrate your successes and acknowledge your defeats, but then move on to the next opportunity and challenge.

—SG

E*ducation's purpose is to replace an empty mind with an open one.*

—MALCOLM S. FORBES

Commit to continuous spiritual, intellectual, and emotional learning. Knowledge has become the key resource in our global economy, and this means it is vital that you commit yourself to *continuous education*. What you know and how quickly you act on it will be the primary factor in your level of achievement.

—SG

For every one of us that succeeds, it's because there's somebody there to show you the way out. The light doesn't necessarily have to be in your family; for me it was teachers and school.

—OPRAH WINFREY

Commit to helping others pursue a better life. Along with committing to your own success, commit to spreading success and enhancing the lives of others, particularly those who are still struggling to find their own way.

The commitments you make to yourself and to others—whether they are individuals or organizations—are the path marks you make on your journey toward your vision of a better life. Every commitment that you fulfill is a goal achieved. When others in your community see that you honor your commitments, they come to perceive you as someone who makes a difference, someone with positive energy who brings success to all aspects of his or her life. Make it a practice to participate in charitable and community organizations. Do it for yourself and for others.   —SG

T*he spirit knows that its growth is the real aim of existence.*

—SAUL BELLOW

››››››››››››

Commit to growing up as a lifelong process. People seem to think that when you reach a certain chronological age, you are a *grown-up*, a finished product, a completed work. Well, it is not so. We all need to grow continuously throughout our lifetimes. We all need to continually seek knowledge and to be always searching for ways to expand our consciousness spiritually, intellectually, and emotionally. We are never grown up. We should always be *growing up*.

—SG